TIMBERLINE

THE LIFE AND TIMES OF FARRELL J. DAVIS

A TRUE STORY

SPECIAL FIRST PRINTING

"COLLECTORS EDITION"

LARGE PRINT

PUBLISHED BY

TIMBERLINE DAVIS

COPYRIGHT © 2012 BY TIMBERLINE DAVIS

ALL RIGHTS RESERVED

No part of this publication may be reproduced, stored in a retrieval system, or transmitted in any form by any means, electronic, mechanical, photocopying, recording, or otherwise, without prior permission.

ISBN: 978-0-9835495-1-2

TIMBERLINE DAVIS

A TRUE STORY

☆ Foreword ☆

We live in a great delightful world filled with love and happiness; yet it is prone to failure, disease, hunger, fear, violence, depressions, war and death.

Having lived in this affable, yet querulous world for a countless number of years, I suppose I must write about the great depression and WW II with insights that are incisive and disarmingly candid.

Someone asked me one day, "Did everybody suffer during the great depression?" I really had no way of knowing, but I believe yes. I must ask. In the dark, are all cats gray? Again, I believe yes.

The Great Depression and WW II happened many long years ago. Those meaningful times are remembered by a few astute individuals but almost forgotten by the young generation of today living a different lifestyle.

The Davis Grandchildren

I have been told that it is a duty for the survivors of those pivotal and epoch making times, to write down an account of that past way of life.

Down through the years I have been hard pressed, by my family, especially my grandkids, to put pencil to paper and write about my life that is fading away every day. They wanted me to write about those distressful depression and war times that I never talk about. Before I get any older and before it becomes too late, they wanted my story.

Farrell Timberline and Juanita Pearl Davis
Celebrating 68 years together.

At my age a cavalcade of clever thoughts and notable memories are not copiously flaunting themselves before me with my porous sieve of a mind.

This book ~13~ is about my life and times from those difficult and perilous days brought back to you as I envisage them, but needless to say, those memories have grown progressively weaker.

When I was young, days and weeks used to drag along in agonizingly slow motion, but now those days and weeks seem to be in a runaway mode.

In this guileful grand scheme of life with its few proud accomplishments and many failures, I am not too old and feeble to write it all down of course, but only to you will I whisper this secret; in my ears the twitter of birds is faint and in my eyes by the day, the sky grows cloudy and dim.

I had many dreams in my life and strived for many advancements and treasures. Some of those dreams came true, but most of them fell by the wayside and never materialized.

Many of you may have traveled down that crooked road and know of what I speak.

I was in every ones way as I lived a precarious 13 years trying to survive in the depression life. That life was full of trials and hardships, yet at times that life was filled with a wealth of happiness and joy. However, those good times were usually crushed down and cancelled out by mountains of lost dreams.

A house where I stayed as a child.

The beginning of WWII brought about a new phase and juncture in my life with that encumbered way of life being changed and reorganized overnight. My life was almost taken away several times but I pulled through.

May this small portion of history, written down here as I remember it, be rewarding and a great reading experience for you and your family.

In this new world we live in today, a world filled with change and opportunity, I believe that almost everyone can search and find the quality life they are seeking.

Farrell Jack Timberline Davis
and
Juanita Pearl Elliott Davis

That fame and fortune you have been searching for, striving and laboring toward, is out there within sight, just waiting for you. I sure hope you can find it.

Sincerely,

Timberline Davis

Dr. Evan Davis and Actor Ben Walker (Davis), Brothers.
My Grandkids grown tall

Chapter 1

The Great Depression

The "great depression" is a story within itself. Back in those appalling, way-worn days, financial gloom was everywhere. People near and far suffered in the throes of that defiling, blatant, far-reaching depression.

A Structure During The Depression

But that being said, we must move on and the depression must share its space with other remembered events, facts and happenings.

"Steal an old man's supper and you do him no disservice."

While trying to write, swirling thoughts come infiltrating through the barrier at the most inopportune times cluttering up normal thought processes.

Coming on through, uncalled for, unwanted and usually bringing to the forefront myriads of old sayings that were cast aside long ago and mostly forgotten.

The old saying that's before me now about stealing an old man's supper, well that was a good saying back in the days of fat, too much plenty and living high on the hog. But during the depression there was no supper to steal, so that old saying's heyday of worth and usefulness has passed.

Grandmother To All

In those hard times all we worried about was where our next meal was coming from. When all of our stomachs were growling, we tightened our belts up a notch; that was breakfast.

Corporal Farrell Davis in Army Air Corps at Miami Beach after transferring from the Army Signal Corps. Just issued a hat and suntan uniform to wear.

Then, moving on and telling about something that happened to your life in the Military, there were so many near-panic things happening to you and on the other hand pleasurable things occurring all the time, it is very hard to keep your thoughts and story on the express track.

Being born and growing up in the Great Depression, I was already walled in with all the bad luck one could get. The number thirteen, superstitions and other warmed over old wives tales were of no significance to me.

Chapter 2

A Rocky Road

Years later when it came time for me to fly my thirteenth bombing mission with the 8th Air Force, the 100th bomb group and the 350th squadron, flying out of Thorpe Abbotts, England, my non-superstitious attitude about the number thirteen abruptly changed.

A B - 17 Damaged In The War

However I'll have to admit to you, my young life was shaped and formed by that great depression. It was a painful, desultory and debasing time.

My Dad lost his job, his land and his house. He went out one day looking for work and I am overburdened to tell you this, he never came back. There is more to say about that of course, but that would call for another book.

Little James is Dead

In our family there were five children. I was the youngest and I am the only one living today.

Mother's favorite child, her dear and precious little boy James, so beautiful and always so friendly, while at play one day was accidentally shot by a playmate.

Hit in the temple with a .22 bullet, he fell to the ground and died instantly. Oh mournful sorrow for all.

It was a sad day for my family and for the neighbors. What was a young grief stricken mother with four hungry and ill clothed children to do? Well, she got a job in the cotton mill working from dawn to dusk. Faultless with helplessness, she let the children go it alone.

We lived with neighbors, relatives and strangers, without full scrutiny and regard.

A Depression Era Home

Chapter 3

Left Behind

I was sent to stay at some places where I stayed with them for only a week. At other places I stayed with them for two or three months.

Why is it that I only retain those memories of bad places while happy places are all forgotten? Maybe because there were so few happy places at that time in my life.

One Sunday we went to visit my Aunt and Uncle. I didn't know that I was being brought along to spend the summer with them. When it came time for us to go home, someone said, "Children go around to the back yard and play."

In the back yard playing I heard the car start up and drive away. I was in a quandary. I ran around to the front to see what was happening. The car with my mother and friends was going back home leaving me behind.

There I was in the middle of the road chasing that car running as fast as I could. I was crying and screaming with my arms outward flaying the air. But the car sped on down the road without me and went out of sight.

At another time in the spring they took me to stay with a rancorous kind of family. The Depression had filled them with bitterness. Why those people agreed to accept me in the first place I don't know. It was plain as day that I wasn't wanted.

After my folks left I was given a bowl of soup to eat. Someone stripped all the hair out of a comb and put a wad of hair in my soup. I couldn't get all the hairs out and I could hardly eat that cold stringy soup.

But all the many circumstances and events that happened while being there were not misapplied; while staying at that dour place, I learned how to grow, learned how to live and learned how to survive.

Many Suffered But Made The Best Of It

When mother took me away to stay someplace, I knew she really wanted me to be somebody and amount to something. Down through the years I've thought about that many times. I've come from nothing and progressed to almost nothing so, Mother would probably be satisfied with me, but then again, perhaps not.

Chapter 4

Little Waif

At one place where I went, I stayed under the bed most of the time. I took naps under there using my arm for a pillow. They never spoke to me while I was under the bed and I enjoyed the bed's protection.

I sometimes sang songs and I learned how to whistle tunes while being under there. Of course to them, while I was out of sight it was good riddance.

At another place where they left me, all of them were loud talkers and scolders. No peace and quietude in that house ever. All of the loudness, loathing and scowls were usually, no totally, directed towards me.

When Mother came back after two or three months to check on me, I was stuttering so badly I couldn't say a single word. When Mother spoke to me, all I could do to answer was nod to her yes or no.

There was one place where I stayed that I believe I almost found ease and solace.

Chapter 5

The Matchbox

One autumn weekend Mother took me way out in the country to stay with some people she knew. After a few days of living with them, those people took me over a hill to visit a neighbor. I was amazed at the neighbor's small matchbox size house but I liked it.

The neighbors were suffering from the depression same as everyone else. They were living in poverty but in those times they didn't even realize it.

With no money to buy food or supplies with, or any thing else needed, they had the inside walls of their house papered with newspapers. What really caught my eye was the front parlor.

It was papered with colored funny papers. It was a beautiful room though, when you backed off and looked at it overall.

Those comic strip pages were held up on the walls with a paste made of flour and water. A fire trap for sure, but papered walls made a house a bit warmer in the cold, rainy and dreary months of winter.

I could hardly wait to go back over and read all of those comics. I was so young that my reading ability was practically nonexistent but I knew lots of words. My reading was good enough for me to read the funnies.

There was a little girl who lived there. She was the same age as me. The little girl only had one dress. Her mother made it from a flour sack that was printed with flowers.

The little girl had beautiful golden curls swinging back and forth across her shoulders. I had to occasionally take a break from reading the funnies to look and marvel at her lovely radiant face. It glowed pink against a white flour sack collar. I don't know why, but I always took time to admire her tender loving smile.

She was an only child and when I came along giving her someone to talk to, her lonely life brightened up considerably. My life brightened up too, but at the beginning of my visits I thought it was just the funny papers doing the brightening.

I would go over there from time to time to read part of a wall. The little girl was so happy when I came. As I read, she followed along behind me talking all the time. I could carry on a conversation with her and read the comics without any trouble. She took a liking to me and looking back, I think she might even have loved me.

Finally I finished reading all of those comic strips and not knowing the reason why, I went back over there and read them all over again.

I liked her too, but at the time I didn't know it.

Chapter 6

We'll Meet Again. . .
Don't know where, don't know when.

In a few weeks Mother came and took me away to another place. I was unable to send any word back to my lovely friend and I suffered with a strange loneliness.

A Nice Car For A Weary Ride.
Destination Unknown.

I was in a predicament for sure and it was wrong for me to go away and not say goodbye to her. There was no way to send word to her. At least, that I could think of.

From that day on, that unpretentious, elegant and devoted little girl was out of my life and gone forever and began fading away from my memory.

When I never returned to read the funnies any more, I know without a doubt what she asked her mother. “Mother, is that all there is? Mother, is that all there is to love?”

Occasionally cherished thoughts, being somewhat akin to homesickness, come unexpectedly upon me from out of nowhere. They hurtle through my mind giving me a disheartened and regretful feeling.

She would find another companion soon. I believe I gave her many memories that would last and cheer her until another friend came along.

If I could, I would like to play those cards differently, but life’s pages cannot be turned back and relived.

I don’t remember the name of that beauty I abandoned. I only remember her golden hair, big blue eyes and all that charm and friendliness.

But I have brought her back from yesterday into today. I have given her a name of my own, *Joan Westbrook*. She now lives and becomes a star in my first fantasy fiction novel, ***THE DAYS OF THE ORG.*** Available at amazon.com.

TIMBERLINE DAVIS
THE DAYS OF THE ORG
A Fantasy Novel

Chapter 7

School Days

When I was six years old, I wanted to go to school more than anything. At the places where I stayed, not one of them wanted to send me. But I was determined and made quite a racket so they let me go.

CANTON

Public Schools

CERTIFICATE OF PROMOTION

THIS CERTIFIES THAT

Has satisfactorily completed the Course of Study prescribed for the Grammar Department of the Canton Public Schools, and is entitled to this Testimonial and to Admission to the High School.

Grade School Diploma

The depression was so bad those folks hardly had any food in the house to eat. They didn't have anything for me to take to school to eat at lunchtime. Once in a while they found an apple on the tree they let me take.

There were no lunchrooms and no free lunches back then. After a few weeks of not eating a lunch, it didn't bother me too much. One good thing about being hungry all day at school, you never got drowsy and fell asleep.

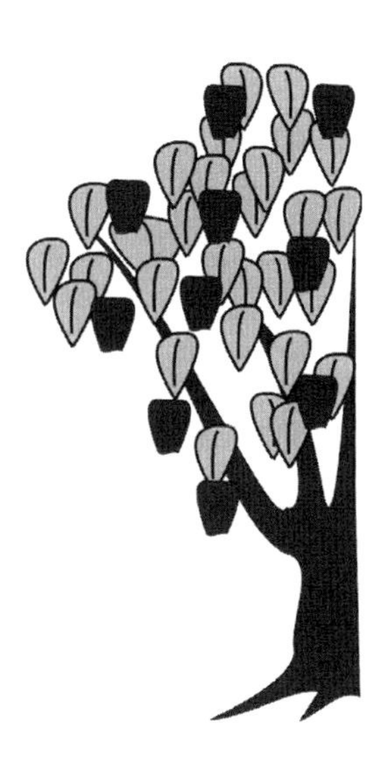

I made all A's up through the sixth grade and I still have those report cards packed in a box in the closet.

Juanita Pearl's Father Growing Up In The Lap of Luxury and Gold Finery

My future wife and her folks were caught in the depression same as my family. She told me that her mother gave her a spoon with a jar of beans to take to school to eat at lunchtime, so she fared pretty well.

Juanita Pearl's Mother and Siblings

Mr. Elliott's family of ten children lived all one fall and winter mostly on beans. In the spring a lady from the government came to bring them some surplus food. She brought bags of beans and put them on the kitchen table. Juanita Pearl and her mother went into the back room and both of them cried over that.

Juanita Pearl's Father During The Depression

Chapter 8

Life Is A Journey, Enjoy the Ride.

The person that said, "Life is a journey, enjoy the ride," must not have lived in the depression. With no shoes to wear until the middle of winter and walking around with feet turned blue from the cold, there was not much enjoyment found in that ride.

When I went to someone's house to eat Sunday dinner with them, I would slip a biscuit into my pocket to eat for breakfast or dinner the next day.

They laughed at me and called me a little "biscuit thief" and today looking back on it I suppose I was. But to me it was my only way of trying to survive and anyway I couldn't take up my belt another notch, because all the notches were already taken up.

The next morning I would take that biscuit and make a hole in it with the tip of my finger and then fill it full of sorghum syrup. That was a mighty fine and enjoyable breakfast for me.

One time when I stayed with an elderly couple, all they had in the kitchen pie safe was salt, lard and flour. The neighbor said we could have all the onions we wanted from his garden. A long row of onions was all he had growing in the garden.

Every day I stirred up flour and water and cooked a big flapjack. And then I fried a pan full of salted onion blades. I ate pretty good that summer.

The old man and woman ate with me and enjoyed my cooking about as much as I did. I'm not sure why, but for some unknown reason they prayed after the meal.

I could write a whole book about my young life in the Great Depression, trying to grow up and trying to live and exist through it all.

Grandmother told me once, "If you try to fail and succeed, which have you done? It's hard to make a comeback when you haven't been any place."

The family hardships, heartbreak and the trying times of long ago would be grievous and sad to write about. Today, everyone, especially children need to know that suffering is going on someplace in the world all the time, day and night. Desperation can strike anyone at any time.

Chapter 9
A Crazy Dream

At the beginning of WW II, on a rainy afternoon, I sat with my friends in the Martha Berry School dormitory in Rome, Georgia. My brain was in a whirl as I tried to figure out what I should do next and where I should go.

Martha Berry School

I was in the front dormitory dayroom. I can still see that 78-rpm record on the player spinning round and round. Harry James and his Orchestra were playing and Helen Forrest was singing. The song was, *I Had The Craziest Dream.*

The reason I mention that song about a crazy dream is because at that time I had a crazy dream myself. At the Berry High School where I was a student, it was the year 1942. Naturally all the talk you could hear from the young men was war talk.

They expected to be drafted into the service soon. When that dreaded notice arrived in the mailbox, they thought it the same as iron shackles. Those shackles would be clamped on them and make prisoners of all.

They talked amongst themselves and all of them day-dreamed about becoming Lieutenants. They wanted to rise above it all and wear gold bars on their shoulders.

Years later, I found out one of those young daydreamers with us that day, rose above it all and did succeed. The young man was working his way through school and searching for a high school diploma the same as I. Later he went into the Service and became a full bird Colonel.

How did all of my other friends in the dormitory with me that day fare? It would be a long time before I found out what happened to all of them.

Chapter 10

Radio Was Grand

Gold bars on my shoulders was an impossible dream for a young teenager like me. But listening to their wild talk, even I got carried away with their daydreams and anxious aspirations.

What was my own crazy dream? Well back then, radio was big and radio was grand. Radio was in my blood and I wanted to go to Ft. McPherson in Atlanta and enter the new radio school that had just opened.

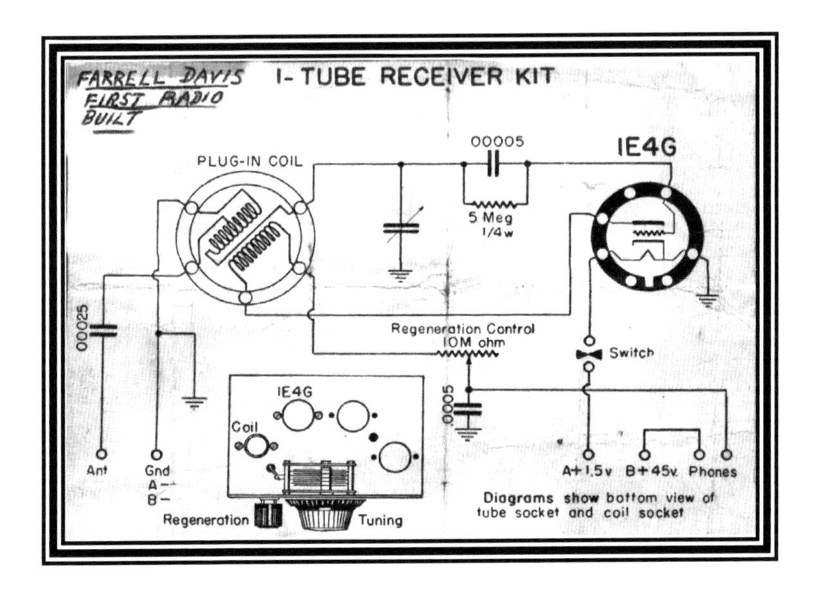

The Schematic Of My First Radio

I agonized over and over about entering that school. Should I go there and enroll?

Was that the proper thing for me to do? I never had anyone to ask or talk to, so good or bad I blindly forged ahead.

Amateur Radio QSL Card

When one stopped and realized that the Draft Board was going to send out draft notices to all of us pretty soon anyway, our thoughts and actions ran counter to our everyday clear rational thinking.

I went over and signed up for the Ft. Mac radio and code school. My schooling was entered into, carried out and diligently fulfilled. I graduated becoming an army radio technician and a high speed radio operator.

About four or five days after graduation, everyone in the class received travel orders. We were ordered to go to the Atlanta train depot to board a train going west. Everyone carried personal belongings in a small handbag. What few belongings I had I carried in my back pocket.

Chapter 11

Army Signal Corps

We were all sent to an Army Signal Corps base and school in Camp Crowder, Missouri for basic training.

Camp Crowder Post Card

Enlisted into the Army was a bewildering and disorienting experience. With no clothes on, we went from one line to another waiting for Doctors to check our physical condition.

We got shots in both arms and were issued shoes, clothing and bedding. The clerk slid a comb and a safety razor across the counter to me. I slid the razor back.

"I won't need the razor, I don't shave."

"Listen Buddy, you go ahead and take the razor, you will need it before long."

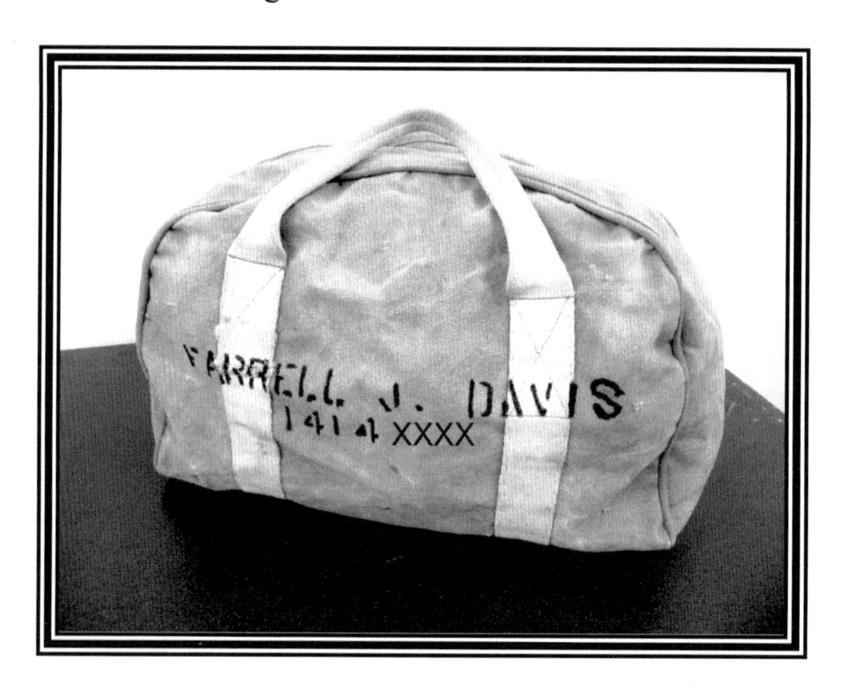

I went ahead and took the razor and sure enough he was right. Much to my surprise, like it or no, before long, just as he told me, I had to start shaving.

Everyone going into the Service was given an army serial number (ASN) that right off you were required to memorize. You might be asked at any time day or night by the higher-ups, "Soldier sound off with your serial number." It was best you didn't forget it.

If you were a draftee and was drafted into the Service, your serial number started with a 3. If you enlisted of your own free will, your number started with a 1.

The serial number was stenciled on your bags, your clothing and on everything you owned…for all to see.

My number started with a 1. There was not another serial number around anywhere starting with a 1 that I could see. Later as you shall see, unforeseen circumstances caused me to become extremely proud of that number and what it stood for.

Enemy In Pursuit At 6:00

Chapter 12

Reveille . . . Not Today

When they want you to leave the barracks and stand formation out in the street, whether in heat, rain or snow, they scream, “Fall out.” I thought it meant, fall out of your bunk and fall out the front door. What did I know? But then as it turned out I was partly right.

About five o’clock the next morning, some crazy guy, I thought, came through the barracks blowing a whistle, turning on lights and yelling at the top of his lungs, “Okay youse guys, get your clothes on and fall out for roll call.”

Everybody jumped out of bed and started putting on their clothes faster than they had ever done before in their entire lives. I just lay still in my bunk and never moved.

The guys would come by my bunk, “Hey get up, we have to fall out, roll call is in two minutes.”

“I’m not going.”

“You don’t have any choice, you have to fall out.”

“I’m not going.”

“Ok, if you don’t fall out it’s your own funeral.”

Pretty soon they marched off to breakfast, chow, and everything got real quiet.

The Sergeant came in. “Are you Davis?”

“Yes.”

B. Davis and F. Davis

"Why are you still in your bunk?"

"Those shots made me sick and I have a fever."

"Do you need to go on sick call?"

"No, after a while I'll be all right."

"Ok, stay in your bunk then."

As it turned out, on my first day in the Army, I slept in my bunk all day. No one believes that crazy story when I tell it. I know it sounds impossible, but it's true.

Chapter 13

Radio School

F. Davis and R. Browne

After basic training, about two or three hundred of us were sent over to a Signal Corps radio school. The radio training was easy for some and tough for others. If you liked radio it was easy.

The Signal Corps issued just about everyone a telegraph/telephone lineman's knife. TL-29, (tool, lineman's). It had a cutting blade and a scraping blade with the end formed into a screwdriver, everything needed to hookup your wires.

TL-29 was stamped on the dark walnut handles on some of them, however, some handles were plain. I think everybody and his brother, all the way from here to Timbuktu has owned and used one of those knives.

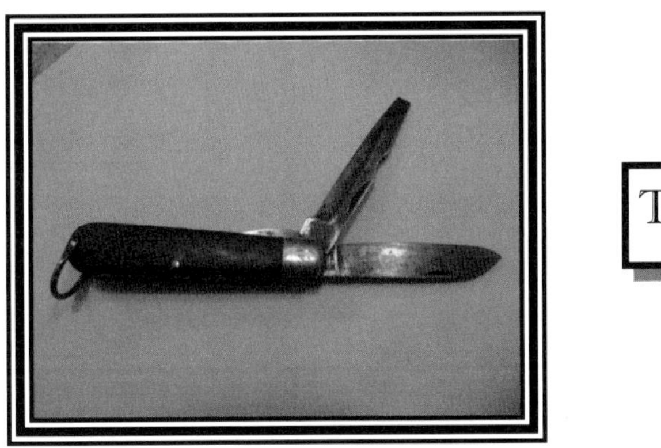

TL - 29

Along with the knife you were issued wire cutters, TL-13. I still have a knife and wire cutters today and they are getting old, but they are still in pretty good shape.

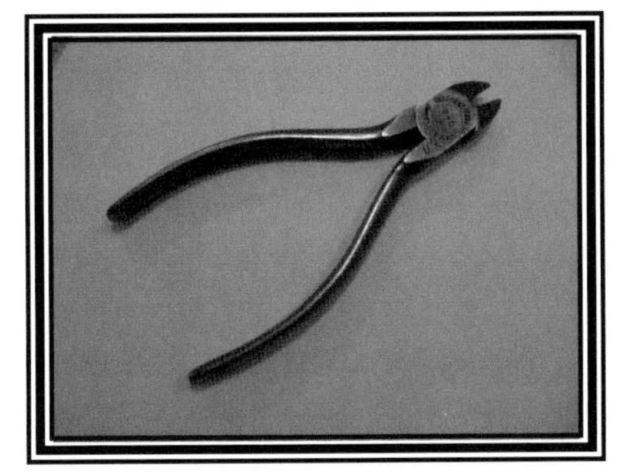

When graduation day rolled around, four students were chosen by the Top Brass to receive promotions. I was still a teen-ager and there were dozens of students who knew radio a lot better that I did.

Working In Audio Lab Today

Chapter 14

Promotion!

Much to my surprise, the Ft. Mac schooling that I had received earlier and the 1 at the beginning of my serial number gave me that edge needed to receive the elusive hard to get promotion.

I was promoted to Corporal and given two stripes to wear on my sleeves. The Corporal stripes on my sleeves at times were good and at other times unsettling.

Every radioman there had dread written on their faces. On some it showed and on others it didn't. Every day radiomen were being shipped out to the foxholes in the South Pacific. They were being sent to replace the wounded and dying soldiers coming back.

About that time the Army Air Corps sent forms to our base and announced they were recruiting men to join the Air Corps. I think every radioman on the base signed up.

I heard some of them talking, "Only one from each section can go, so we don't really have a chance."

They were right about that. Almost no one had a chance, and they didn't get to go.

That night as I lay on my bunk thinking everything through, I thought to myself, here I am a teen-age Corporal. The Air Corps just might be interested in a quirky young guy like me.

I really liked the Signal Corps and didn't want to leave it. I didn't know exactly what to do. I had no one to ask and no one to talk to, so I decided to go down in the morning and look into that Air Corps thing.

The next morning I went to the day room, as the office was called, and filled out some Air Corps papers.

Believe it or not, in the middle of the next week, there I was on a train, all alone, with all my bags, clothes and belongings, traveling to the south.

I was now in the Air Corps and the train, with a change in Atlanta, was headed for Miami Beach, Florida.

Life at Miami Beach in the Air Corps was great if you call elation one moment and super-stress the next moment, great. It was such a beautiful place though and had such delightful weather I really enjoyed being there.

Calisthenics on the beach every day with a swim in the ocean afterwards was great.

One day a flustered young man walked over to the window and rammed his fist through the glass. They took him to the clinic and the Doctor sewed up his hand.

By then I had already learned, you've got to ride with the tide and don't let that big wave swamp you.

I was down in Florida quite a while. I was taking Air Corps basic training while waiting for my slot up the line to open up, whatever that slot was. Many mind boggling incidents and happenings and lots of study and work paraded before me in Florida.

Life In The Army Air Corps

Chapter 15

Missouri 307 CTD

Davis, Long and a Friend

Over in the placement section they saw that I was one that needed more schooling. I could have told them that.

They sent about a hundred of us called "Squadron D", to the University of Missouri, the 307th Air Corps CTD (College Training Detachment).

I wished I could have gone to the Berry College CTD, which was CTD 1, but I suppose you've heard the old adage, "If wishes were horses, beggars would ride."

Going to Missouri was a move that I liked and it was also a momentous turning point in my life.

Living Quarters at University of Missouri

My grades were good, but my flight training in a Piper Cub was bad. We had to fly straight up until the airplane stalled then fell back tail first toward earth. My stomach tried to stay up there not wanting to fall out of the sky. My stomach wanted to throw up but I calmed it down and held it in check.

The Flight Instructor was too wild and reckless for me. One day he came flying back in with telephone wires dangling from the Piper Cub wheels. They gave him a good talking to, but he never changed.

Studying At Missouri University

Chapter 16

Dining Hall Queen

There was a lady with bright red hair in charge of the dining hall. She was very pretty and was the Star of the dining hall and Queen of the Air Corps students. Back then I thought she was real old, but now as I look back, I realize she was only about 25 or 35.

The first day I walked into the dining hall, I saw her about the same time she saw me. Her face lit up and she came over and spoke to me.

Juanita Pearl Elliott

"Young man, where are you from?"

"Georgia."

She became a dear friend and confidant.

"Georgia, if you need extra food just call on me."

Every time I walked into the dining hall, she would yell out across the room, "Hello Georgia."

I never figured out why she took a liking to me, I think I might have reminded her of someone from her earlier days, but I'm not sure. She never told me anything about her life, back when she was a teenager in school.

One day I went over and whispered to her, "That new girl working at the food counter is the most beautiful girl I have ever seen in my whole life."

"Even prettier than me?

"Well not quite, but almost."

"That young lady is Juanita Pearl Elliott, do you want me to get you a date with her?"

"Do you think you could?"

"Sure, Georgia, just leave it to me."

Well, she got me a date with that beauty and what happened to us later turned out good.

The Most Beautiful Girl I Have Ever Seen

Chapter 17

Graduation

Squadron D as we were called, graduated from the University of Missouri, Air Corps 307th CTD. We received our diplomas and then shipped out.

University of Missouri

Columbia

This is to certify that

FARRELL J. DAVIS

has successfully completed the program of courses prescribed by the U. S. Army Air Forces and conducted by the University of Missouri for the 307th College Training Detachment (Aircrew), and that his academic record in these courses is on file with the Registrar of the University.

Columbia, Missouri, January 10, 1944

SIGILL. UNIVERSITATIS MISSOURIENSIS MDCCCXXXIX

At the placement center in Texas, there was a shortage of navigators and radiomen. They had more men than they needed for pilots and the other positions. Just about everybody down there wanted to be a pilot.

There was a grave shortage of radiomen that could send and receive International Morse Code, a specialty which was listed in another category altogether.

It took concentration and special training before a radioman could tune in an International Morse Code signal (cw) on the radio and then write down on paper what those dots and dashes coming in a mile-a-minute were saying. It took a lot of patience and a lot of practice before a radio technician could do that.

With my radio operator training that gave me my Corporal stripes, I didn't figure that I would be sent to aircraft mechanic's school, cook and baker's school or anything else.

I almost knew that I was going to be assigned to radio and that's exactly what happened to me. My longtime radio dreams were falling into place.

Amateur Radio QSL Card

Chapter 18

13 Hours - Boy To Man

Before long a notice was posted on the bulletin board. We were notified that we were going to a radio school in Sioux Falls, South Dakota.

Being a radio operator on the battlefield and being a radio operator in an airplane are different specialties and require different kinds of training.

Radio Operator 'Aircrew' Silver Wings

Early on a Monday morning after going to breakfast and returning to the barracks, we were called to fall out.

We were in several formations out in front of the barracks with our barracks bags lying on the street beside us. Trucks were standing by to take us to the railroad depot. Today we were shipping out to Sioux Falls.

A Captain and two Sergeants stood before us. A Sergeant's voice called out in the semi-darkness, "Corporal Davis step forward."

I never moved. I expected to see another Corporal Davis step out, but there was no other.

A bit louder this time, “Corporal Davis step forward.” I knew this time they were calling me.

I know nothing about travel. I know nothing about troop trains. Being a radioman is all I know. Why are they calling me?

I then walked to the front and saluted the Captain. “Are you Corporal Davis?”

“Yes, Sir.”

“Corporal Davis you are in charge of the troop train. My Sergeants will see you to the railroad station.”

“Yes, Sir.”

Right then I thought, “Yesterday I was only a boy, today I am a man.”

Chapter 19

Troop Train

They handed me several large envelopes containing orders, records, my instructions, a list of restaurants and a book of meal tickets.

We got on the trucks, rode to the station and boarded the train. Pretty soon the train pulled out and we were on our way. It is a long ride traveling on a slow troop train all the way from Texas to South Dakota.

I didn't know if I could handle this or not because I was just a boy turned man in thirteen hours. I had only shaved twice. The first time I shaved was on a Monday and the second time was on the following Monday.

Everything went along smoothly for me. All the soldiers respected my two stripes. They were orderly and quiet when we went into restaurants to eat. So as we traveled northward, I had no trouble with them.

I managed to stay ahead of trouble, almost. When we stopped in Omaha, Nebraska, our train ride and our good luck took a serious nose dive. The railroad took away our train and sent it out on another run.

I was told that they would have another train for us at noon on Saturday, but Saturday was three days away. I had to come up with something and come up with it fast.

Photo courtesy of Springfield Underground

"What happened to us when the engine ran off the tracks one night at midnight?"

Chapter 20

A Three Day Pass

The Military Police in the terminal were helpful, but they kept a close eye on us. I went into their office.

"We have been delayed. Do you think it would be all right if I gave everybody on my train a three-day pass?"

"Corporal, they are your men and it is your train, you can do whatever you want."

I wrote out passes and gave everyone a three-day pass. I told them, "Our train will leave Omaha Saturday at twelve noon. Without fail, all of you be back by then."

I could go on and on with this. Did we get another train? Did all the men get back in time? What happened to us when the engine ran off the track one night at midnight? Did anyone get hurt?

Way up there in the north please know, we had all kind of adventures on that arduous train ride before we reached our destination, Sioux Falls, S.D.

It was mighty cold when we arrived at our radio school up in Sioux Falls, but we managed.

Later when we graduated the weather was warm and we had found Sioux Falls to be a nice place.

Chapter 21

Gunnery School

Next for us came an aerial gunnery school at a Yuma, Arizona Air Force Base. Sweating on the ground and freezing in the air, we were trained on the operation and firing of aircraft .50 caliber machine guns.

Air Corps Silver Gunnery Wings

Upon completion of gunnery training, I received silver gunner's wings and I was now ready to join a flight crew and get prepared to go overseas. In the 100th Bomb Group I wore the Radio Operator wings.

They gave me a few days leave to go home and say goodbye to my folks. I thought to myself, "My training is almost over. I am getting close to the war now."

Chapter 22

Memphis Blues

I called my beautiful girl friend in Missouri, the same girl that the red headed lady in the dining hall got me a date with. I invited her to go to Georgia with me to see my family. She enjoyed travel and excitement.

She had been picking cotton close to her home and had enough money for a train ticket. She hated to spend all the money she had, but she reluctantly accepted and would go with me.

Our plans were made to meet in the Memphis train terminal on Sunday at 12 noon. Bad news all around, my train from Yuma to Memphis was delayed.

Sunday noon passed by. Monday noon went on by. I was still far away traveling on a slow train, but I was getting closer all the time. Noon on Tuesday passed by. By then I was beginning to get worried.

Was my girl friend still in the terminal waiting? Did she go back to Missouri? Where could she be by now?

Early Wednesday morning I was still rolling along and getting very anxious, I thought to myself, "What have I done?" I have really messed up good this time.

I was helpless because I couldn't help what the railroad did. But would she ever talk to me again or see me again? There was nothing left for me to do but remain calm, sit down and wait and see.

Memphis Train Terminal

Chapter 23

Through Thick & Thin

The train finally arrived in Memphis. I hurried into the terminal not knowing what to expect. It was crowded and I anxiously looked up and down the rows of seats.

I saw a beautiful girl sitting in a seat out in the middle of the terminal. It was she. She was asleep. She had been sitting there three days and nights waiting for me.

Walking over, I was looking at her clothes, all wrinkled. I could see that she was tired and weary.

Waiting Room At Train Station

As I walked over to where she was sitting I said to myself, "That Juanita Pearl is a girl that will stick with you through thick and thin. I had better latch onto her at my first golden opportunity." Folks that's just what I did.

This past Christmas the year of 2011 was our 67th Christmas together. There is a lot more to be told about our travels down the crooked road of life. Those adventures with good times and bad times, success and failure, would fill at least a 400 page book.

Our Young Family
with
Barry and Greg

Chapter 24

Aircrew Training

Sometime later I was assigned to a flight crew of nine airmen.

Bombardier 1st Lt. Walter M. Gibson, Pilot 2nd Lt. Milton Alvo, Co-pilot 2nd Lt. David C. Tallichet, Navigator 2nd Lt. Donald E. Israel, Armorer S/Sgt. George I. Murray, TTE T/Sgt. Boleslaw V. Bitel, ROG T/Sgt. Farrell J. Davis, BTG S/Sgt. Woodrow W. Wilson, TG S/Sgt. Leonard G. Woodruff.

We spent several weeks flying practice missions training as an aircrew. We were stationed at Hunter Field, Savannah, Ga. and at an AFB near Gulfport, Miss.

On a high altitude training flight one day it was very cold, about -30 degrees below zero. My oxygen regulator froze and was not working properly. I was not getting enough oxygen to breathe and I began to feel light headed with a floating sensation.

I called the pilot. “I’m feeling bad and I’m about to pass out. I think I’m going to die.”

“Hold on, I’ll send somebody back to check on you.”

The co-pilot ran back to the radio room but by that time I was having convulsions and had already fallen out of my radio chair. My body was drawn up and growing stiff and cold.

Photo courtesy of Larry Simeone

My Ride To The Hospital

The co-pilot knew exactly what was wrong with me. He grabbed my oxygen hose and connected the hose to a walk-around oxygen bottle giving me plenty of oxygen to breathe and that saved me. In about two more minutes it would have been too late. I'd have been gone.

The next thing I knew I was in a hospital bed somewhere near New Orleans and the B-17 with the flight crew was gone. I really liked that aircrew and I was so afraid they would go on to England without me.

Going To England

Chapter 25

AT - 6 Texan

In a few days a soldier flying a single engine airplane, an AT-6 Texan, came for me and took me back to my home base.

I arrived there just in time. It seemed my luck had changed for the better. They were still in training, flying missions. They thought they might never see me again. With smiles all around, they welcomed me back.

100th Bomb Group Aircraft

We were scheduled to pick up a brand-new B-17 four-engine bomber and deliver it to England. But before we left we had to go to the base hospital and get some shots that were required before going into foreign countries.

We got our shots and also the Doctors checked us over. The Dentist told me that I had four wisdom teeth that were going to cause trouble flying at high altitudes and he wanted me to come back to the dental office first thing the next morning.

"Corporal, those wisdom teeth have got to come out."

I had rather find someone's cut off finger in my bowl of soup than get those teeth pulled, but I had no choice. Like the Dentist said, "I knew they were coming out."

They had to dig those four teeth out and my gums and jaws were sore for a long time. I was half sick from those shots and half sick from my sore mouth. I'm trying to tell you that I was feeling downright bad.

I caused about a three or four-day delay but soon we went over and received a new B-17. The next day or two following, we were on our way to England.

Chapter 26

Bad Weather

They didn't turn us loose to go on our own merry way. I had a packet of orders and instructions with radio station frequencies that were for Morse Code position reports. Every minute of our flight was being watched over. We were in a war but also still in training.

Our route of travel was New Jersey, Bangor, Maine, Goose Bay, Labrador, Greenland, Keflavik, Iceland and the British Isles.

The weather was really bad when we landed at Bangor. The runways were snow covered. I am not exaggerating when I say the snowdrifts at Bangor went from the sidewalk up to the tip-top of the houses. I had never seen anything like that before in my whole life.

When we landed at an Air Force Base at Keflavik, Iceland, we had to wait there two weeks. Bad weather was ahead of us. Finally, we continued on and turned in the new airplane to the proper authorities. We were sent to a placement center awaiting assignment.

Chapter 27

"Bloody Hundredth"

Headquarters

We were assigned to the 8th Air Force, 100th Bomb Group, 350th squadron. I think everybody in England had heard about the "Bloody Hundredth" Bomb Group, located in the countryside in and around Thorpe Abbotts.

Memories Of Thorpe Abbotts

Everyone had a story to tell and the stories I heard sounded bad, if you call many airplanes exploding and falling out of the sky, bad. However, no one on our crew was bothered in any way about the Bloody Hundredth's notoriety. We gave it no more thought. In fact, we were proud, scared and apprehensive, maybe, but proud to be in the 100th.

I wish I had the space here to write about all those incredible tales that were told to us. Whether those tales were true or not didn't bother us. We had other things closer at hand to think about. We rode a train to a small town by the name of Diss. A waiting truck took us from Diss into the 100th Bomb Group air base located at Thorpe Abbotts.

Not Everyone Had A Good Touchdown.

After settling in, we had to fly a few training missions before going into combat.

Quarters - Thorpe Abbotts

100th BG Service Area

Chapter 28

Training Missions

Flying training missions or real missions was almost an everyday occurrence.

Finest Men In The Air Corps

On a training flight one day, we flew from our base in Thorpe Abbotts northward and landed at Crumlin AFB in Belfast, Ireland.

There was a store nearby where we could buy souvenirs. Not being a rich Belgravian type of guy, I looked at brass items instead of silver and gold ones, hoping I had enough money to buy the brass.

Monkey Doorknocker

I found a brass doorknocker that I liked and thought that I might buy. The owner of the store was old and throughout his many years of selling had perfected his salesman spiel. He came on strong.

"Son, that doorknocker is filled with wonder-works of magic. Straight out of mythology it comes to you. It will protect your life forever no matter where you are. When fastened to your door, it will fearlessly guard your home and frighten off intruders and thieves."

I thought to myself then, "That graying old gentleman learned how to sell by selling snow cones to Eskimos."

I bought that evil looking doorknocker and kept it with me throughout the war. I put it in a sock and kept it hidden away in the bottom of my B-4 bag. I never thought about it again until I returned home after the war was over. It was a treasured, but haunting, souvenir.

Years later I mounted it on the back door of my house. I wish I had the space here to tell you about the uncanny chain of events and all the things that happened to that house. It was quite unbelievable, yet fascinating as tall scary tales go.

Chapter 29

Stray Bullet

At Thorpe Abbotts on our third or fourth day, someone lying on his bottom bunk was checking over his pistol. It was a .45 automatic and it fired accidentally. The bullet went through the upper bunk and out through the roof.

The loud bang caused a great commotion. Everybody from all around came into the barracks to see if anyone got shot. An Officer came in and when he found out no one got hurt. He was so relieved that he laughed.

“You guys be careful in here. I’ll have to call the English and get someone to come over and patch the hole in the roof. Don’t be waving those guns around in the barracks. This is not the Wild West. Leave your guns over in your lockers until you go on a mission.”

The lucky young man assigned to the top bunk was coming back from the toilet to his top bunk when the gun went off. He missed getting shot and killed by one minute. Possibly, that one minute in his life was as good to him as one thousand years.

Chapter 30

Mission No. 1

Flying A Mission

Mission No. 1. Finally the big day of going on a mission arrived for our crew.

Our pilot and all the crewmember's names were listed on the next day's mission chart. Time to sweat I suppose. Good or bad, in the morning we were going on our first mission.

Our crew was normally quite talkative, but for the rest of the day hardly a word was spoken. The next day we were going out and for sure we would be tested.

I wondered how we would fare the first time out, coming under fire. There was a lot of unease and anxiety on our part and of course many surprises lying in wait for us out there in the unknown. We were well trained though, so our confidence was high.

When on the ground, I wore a Royal Air Force insignia on my cap. It was given to me by a friend in the RAF. He was pleased that I wore it.

Someone got us awake and out of bed about 3:30 a.m. the next morning. We went in a truck to the mess hall to eat breakfast. At 3:30 in the morning my stomach is woozy and turning summersets.

If you were going on a mission you got fried eggs and ham. Everybody else got powdered eggs. They were frying eggs on a big stove right before you.

"How many eggs for you?"

"Just one over easy and no ham."

"What's the matter you got a bad tooth?"

"No but I've got four sore gums."

"Ok here's your egg, grab yourself a cup of that hot coffee over there."

"I don't drink coffee."

"Why not?"

"When I grew up we didn't have any coffee, so I never learned to drink it."

"Ok, there's a glass of powdered milk over there."

I ate my egg and drank some cold milk to wash it down with and wash out my mouth. From that early breakfast my stomach objected with a *tilt*. I felt a lot better afterwards, even almost good, and I moved on.

Clockwise: F.J. Davis (with insignia on cap), L.G. Woodruff, G.I. Murray, W.W. Wilson, B.V. Bitel

Chapter 31

Target for Today

We went into a British Nissan hut for our briefing. All of us called them Quonset huts, (first manufactured in Quonset, R.I.). We couldn't tell any difference between the huts. A hut was just a hut to us.

MP guards standing at the door were checking IDs before anyone was admitted into the restricted Nissan briefing hut.

F.J. Davis

In the far end of the cigarette smoke filled room, a big map was on the wall covered over with a curtain. There was a ribbon on the map running from our base at Thorpe Abbotts to the target. The targets were usually someplace in Austria, Germany, Czechoslovakia or France.

When the curtain was pulled back, you usually could hear groans, oh no's and other kinds of language, because just about every target was bad.

Later, I found out that anyone who has experienced fear in combat could understand the feelings everyone had when they first looked at the target map.

100th Bomb Group Headquarters
Aerial View

Chapter 32

Hard Work

Secret orders, instructions, codes, radio frequencies, secret recall phrase, etc. were given to the pilot, co-pilot, navigator, bombardier and radioman.

My radio orders sheet was called a flimsy. The secret information for radio was printed on rice paper. To keep the secret information from falling into enemy hands if the plane crash landed in enemy territory or if you ditched in the channel or a lake, the radioman was required to wad the paper up and eat it.

We had to put on a lot of rigging before flying at high altitude. The bitter cold up there at high altitude was –10 to occasionally –50 degrees.

Someone from another crew down the way called flying with bottled oxygen and flying at –40 degrees below zero, living within the jaws of death. Boy, he sure got that right.

Dynamotor removed from a shortwave radio receiver

We had an electrically heated suit, with electric boots and electric gloves. There's only 24 to 28 volts in a B-17 but there's lots of it and plenty for everything. How does 24 volts power the equipment? The answer, of course, is by using dynamotors. Inside my radio receiver was a dynamotor that converted 24 volts into 220 volts. Other pieces of equipment had dynamotors that provided the necessary voltages needed there.

We put on an aviators cap with built in headphones, a throat microphone, oxygen mask and goggles that were used to keep your tears from freezing.

We had our pistols, .45 caliber automatics, on our belts hanging at our side.

We had a flak jacket and a tapered sporran flak apron to protect vital parts and another flak apron in our chair to sit on. We put on a parachute harness and strapped a bailout bottle of oxygen on our leg. A pea size compass was carried in each pocket and several were hidden away in the lining of our clothes. One was used to find your way back to the front lines of battle in case you crash landed or had to bail out over enemy territory.

We never had to bail out. On one mission we had lots of smoke in the plane and we got the override call, "Prepare to bailout and stand by your open door."

With our chutes on and our oxygen hoses connected to walk around bottles, we went and stood by an open door. Someone yelled, "You can't jump out that door, the wind will blow you back in. You've got to dive out."

I thought I knew all about stress until then. We waited in line by the door for what seemed like an eternity, then finally we received another call. "Pilot to crew, trouble averted, go back to positions."

Flying In Formation

Chapter 33

Throwing Out Chaff

Usually the last piece of equipment we put on before the mission was our Mae West life preserver, inflated by mouth. I always wanted to inflate mine to see if it really looked like Mae West, but I never got that chance, for which I am thankful.

After getting dressed with all our rigging, every crew-member went to his position and checked out his equipment. In addition to my radio position check out, I had a .50 caliber machine gun back in the aircraft's waist that I checked out.

Radio Operator At Machine Gun

I had boxes of chaff that I stacked in the radio room next to the chaff chute in the floor. Chaff was a strip of aluminum foil folded at an angle. It came in bundles and each foil angle in the bundle was about the size of a soda straw and looked like an “L” .

The chaff chute in the floor acted like a vacuum cleaner. The suction would grab that bundle of chaff in your hand and all you had to do was turn it loose and it was gone on its way.

Chaff floating in the air, spinning round and round reflected a signal back to the enemy’s radar receivers aiming those big anti-aircraft guns below. You hoped the floating chaff was giving them a false reading.

The navigator called me when it was time to throw out chaff. I had to work like crazy to get it all thrown out in time, but I always made it.

The enemy had about 50 to 1500 guns guarding each target city. I heard someone say there were about 2500 guns ringed around Berlin, maybe even more.

Chapter 34

Fighting The War

At prearranged times the pilot or co-pilot called out for a crew check. We always answered in this order, "Navigator ok." "Bombadier ok." "Engineer ok." "Radio ok." "Armorer ok." "Ball turret ok." "Tail gunner ok." That procedure checked out your oxygen supply, your throat microphone, headphones and interphone control box.

After our first morning crew check nothing more was said and the pilot taxied out and got into line waiting for his turn to takeoff. There was radio silence and the crew members in the nose of the plane were watching for a green light and/or a green-green flare signaling your turn for takeoff.

Early Morning Takeoff

For everybody on board, takeoff was an anxious time. Soon, we got the green light and flare, and pulled out. The wheels of that loaded down plane began rolling along the runway. "It was now or never," I thought.

The British had radio beacon transmitters scattered across the region. Those transmitters emitted signal beams straight up into the air. B-17s circled around the beams to get into position and to climb to a designated altitude.

Those radio beacon sites were called Bunchers and Splashers.

There was a Splasher radio beacon in a field off the end of one of the runways at the 100th bomb group airfield. It was called Splasher 6. The planes circled around the radio Buncher and Splasher beacon signals forming into squadrons, groups and wings.

When flying around in the local area on a training flight, if the airport got socked in, the Splasher 6 radio beacon at Thorpe Abbotts could be used if needed.

Chapter 35

Eighth Air Force

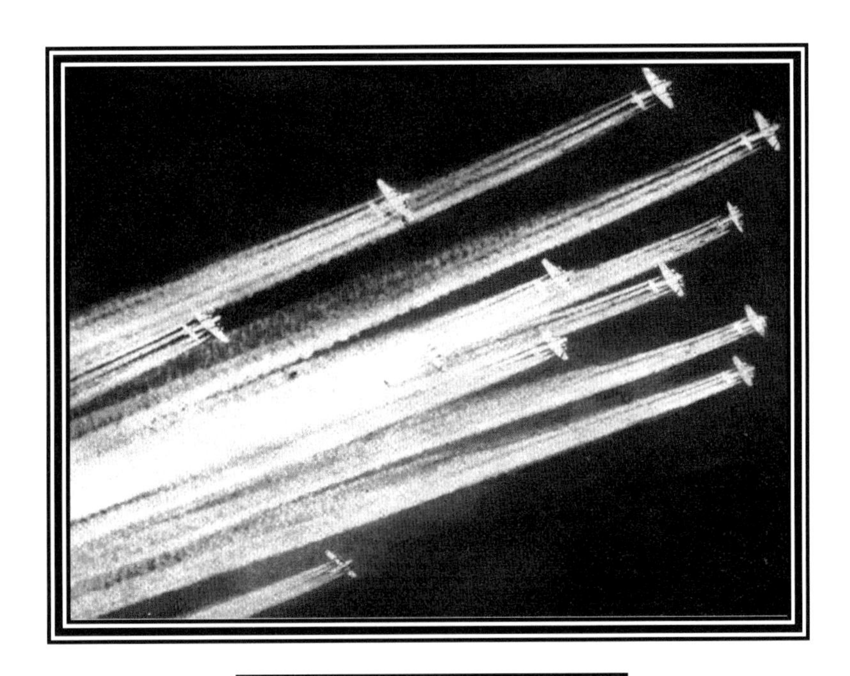

Instrument Of Warfare

When the mighty Eighth Air Force of 800 to 1800 aircraft was assembled into a 100 mile long column and headed out toward the enemy to destroy them, I believe it was the most feared instrument of warfare ever devised.

With its thousands of machine guns for protection and thousands of bombs ready to rain down, millions of the enemy down under that giant armada trembled with fear.

There was no place for the enemy to hide. A basement or storm shelter offered no protection. The roof of a house or barn was like paper. Their waking hours were filled with cringing terror.

Radio Operator Watching Bombs Fall
From The Bomb Bay

In this war they never knew when a bomb might hit out in the front yard and blow them out of bed or away from the dinner table. The target could be missed due to clouds and winds and a string of bombs could go across any village or farm. In the middle of an air war down below is not a good place to be. Upstairs was not too safe either, I might add.

Chapter 36

Raining Iron

Also when the big anti-aircraft shells being fired at the planes overhead exploded about four or five miles high in the air, jagged pieces of iron fell down everywhere on the countryside.

If a bomb didn't blow you to bits, a chunk of iron on the heads of people working out in the fields could kill them.

The enemy knew that soon, where they manufactured guns and ammunition could be visited from the sky. Then, the only thing they were sure of was death.

Bomb Bay Doors Open

We made it through that first mission okay. If I remember correctly, our bomb load that day was 36 one hundred pound bombs.

We were on the bomb run and I opened the door to the bomb bay. I watched the bombs fall and also watched bombs exploding on the target below from groups up ahead. The bombs rapidly dropped out one at a time ticking back and forth, falling out from one side of the bomb bay racks then the other.

As soon as all the bombs were gone, I went on interphone override and told everyone, "All the bombs are gone, bomb bay clear."

"Bombs are gone, bomb bay clear."

In the movies they always said "Bombs away" but I never said that.

At that time the bomb bay doors began to close and the pilot put one wing straight down making a sharp turn and at the same time falling to a lower altitude. It was a maneuver used to get out of the damaging flak at the bomb run altitude and to move away from certain destruction.

Everybody on the plane had been waiting hours for that one moment to arrive. Almost immediately, all the planes in our 350th squadron began to assemble again at the rally point (RP). This was for our protection and for the flight back to Thorpe Abbotts, the base of the 100th Bomb Group.

Photo courtesy of Dr. J. Howard Cobble

100th BG Control Tower At Thorpe Abbotts

Chapter 37

Regular Missions

Photo Courtesy Of Elma Fay

Back on the ground at Thorpe Abbotts, we went over to the Red Cross van. They gave each crewmember a shot of whiskey and a cup of orange juice. I didn't drink so I traded my whiskey to another crewmember for his cup of orange juice. After flying all day two paper cups of orange juice tasted really good and refreshing to me.

We began to fly regular missions going out every three or four days, and sometimes every day.

Squadrons Of The Bloody 100th

We flew in several different B-17s. Not all of them had a name painted on the side of the nose. We flew some missions in "Baby Bunty" and "Skipper II," Most of our missions were flown in a new plane that we claimed for our own, named "Spirit of Pittwood."

350th Squadron Returning After A Mission

We knew the plane didn't really belong to us. I tried to find out where the name "Spirit of Pittwood" came from, but I never found out.

Baby Bunty

Grand Old Airplane

Chapter 38

No Bastion

One day a young kid from another aircrew came over to me and asked me a question. I was mighty young at the time but he was even younger.

“Did the all seeing God put me into all this pain, suffering and fear?”

“No I don’t believe God did, I think evil men did it.”

“If God did, do you think God will get me out of it?”

“Yes, if He actually put you into it, I believe He will somehow get you out of it alive and well.

Not being a bastion of Biblical knowledge I didn’t know how to answer his questions.

The Plane We Claimed As Our Own

While growing up, the folks that I stayed with during the depression were not church going people. In the evening with only a lamp in the kitchen to see by and with two or three hungry babies crying, they were too tired and weary to try to read the Bible.

Most of those people I stayed with long ago lived along Ga. highway 61 and Ga. highway 5. Those highways were both dirt roads back then. They were muddy with deep ruts and hard to travel over.

Churches were few and far between with only one service a month. The Church doors were never locked but sometimes it would be months before the Preacher came back to preach.

Our times going to church back in those days were also few and far between. So you can easily see that I knew very little about the Bible.

Down through the centuries of man's striving to live, to adjust and to become civilized, warfare has always been commonplace. Did God start the wars or just permit them to happen? You will have to ask someone smarter than I am for the answer to that question.

Chapter 39

A Woeful Day

A few days later we were flying on a mission and someone called out on interphone override to all the crew, "Look at that plane!"

B - 17 Going Down In Flames

I looked out my window and saw a B-17 from our group going down in a flat spin. Then it nosed down and flew straight down toward the earth. No parachutes were seen coming out of the plane. Chutes were hardly ever seen coming from a plane spinning around. Sometimes there would be one or two chutes.

Bomb Run Flak

The plane exploded into a big cloud of black, gray and white smoke all lit up from within with an orange glow.

I found out when we got back to Thorpe Abbotts, that my young friend's pain, suffering and fear had ended.

On one mission I was at my waist gun trying to get a shot at one of the many enemy fighters coming toward us from out of the sun. Every gun on our aircraft was firing. Looking into the sun on that mission weakened my eyes. They are still weak, even now. Today when I look at a power pole standing out in a field, half way down on that pole I see a gash like this, >.

About all of the enemy fighters that flew up close and within range of our machine guns were shot full of holes. As they streaked on by, our .50 caliber guns smoked them and turned some of them into flying scrap metal.

As long as there were straggler B-17s with engine trouble flying alone outside the formation though, the enemy fighters swarmed around them instead of us and shot them full of holes, usually knocking them out of the sky. Flying alone was suicide.

At times you could hear big shells exploding underneath the plane. On one occasion holes were being made in the floor all around me. I was expecting a piece of flak to come up my pants leg at any moment. Most of the holes in the floor were about the size of a quarter but one of them was as large as a baseball.

On every mission we flew straight and level on the bomb run for about five minutes or more. We were in an extremely dangerous situation and position at that time.

Even though our B-17 airplane was shot and blasted full of holes on that particular mission, we dropped our bombs without any trouble and completed the mission.

Chapter 40

100 Flak Holes

When we got on the ground at Thorpe Abbotts, we counted 100 holes in the airplane and there were a lot more holes that we didn't count. All of that flak iron going through the plane didn't hit anything important enough to put us out of commission.

I think we were all too young and too busy to be afraid. However, on the times when we were about one second away from death, we had tremendous fear.

I found out that men and machines work a whole lot better at a temperature of 40 degrees than at –40.

Many a time at 40 below, I wanted to turn the heat in my suit higher and wished the heat control knob had another notch on it. But the heat was blistering my stomach the way it was.

Everyone on our crew was awarded the Air Medal and our promotions came through. Now, I had four stripes on my sleeves.

We completed mission number 12 and everybody in the barracks was lamenting the fact and worrying for us about our mission number 13 coming up. I was worried, of course, but I laughed at them and gave it not one moment of thought.

ROG F. Davis & BTG W. Wilson With Air Medal "Woodrow W. Wilson Died Nov. 1997"

Night follows day and day follows night. The 13th mission finally arrived. We got up early and went to breakfast the same as always.

Bombs On Target

Chapter 41

Thirteenth Mission

We went to our 13th briefing and when the curtain was pulled back exposing that big map and showing the target, not much was said. Was that good or bad? My mind racing back and forth didn't know what to think.

We went about our work at the airplane. I suppose everyone had forgotten that this was our 13th mission, because nothing was said about it.

Flying At Minus Forty Degrees

I looked in the bomb bay and what I saw in there didn't surprise me. The target given to our group that day was a big canal with submarine pens.

We had six one thousand pound bombs loaded in the bomb bay. The B-17 we were flying that day was the "Spirit Of Pittwood." It was a great flying airplane and I knew it could handle it, but then every plane has a bad day once in a while.

It was a long flight and it sure was cold on that April day. I had my heated suit control turned way up on high. But soon I had a lot of things other than shivering to think about. The pilot made a call on interphone override, "Pilot to crew, we have an engine out."

We flew along for a while and I wondered if we were going to make a bomb run with one engine out. Right away my questioning thoughts received an answer.

"Pilot to crew we have another engine out, supercharger trouble, we are turning back."

I called the pilot. "Radio to pilot."

"Go ahead radio."

"The engine's super-charger amplifier is back here in the radio room and I have a spare unit, do you want me to put the spare unit in?"

"Yes radio, go ahead, we'll give it a try."

My fingers were so cold that I could hardly get the safety wire untwisted and the knurled nuts holding the unit in the rack loosened, but I finally got that done and got the black box changed.

"Radio to pilot, the spare unit is installed."

"Okay radio, I'll see if I can get that engine started."

Insignia Collected Along The Way

After a few minutes, "Pilot to crew, I got an engine started and we are going back to the base on three engines. Radio, call British anti-aircraft radio and get us permission to enter the country."

Chapter 42

Call To British Radio

We were a long way from England so I let the trailing wire antenna out. It had a big heavy cast iron egg on the end to hold it down. That iron egg kept it down away from the airplane and kept it from swinging back and forth, wrapping itself around the tail of the airplane.

I liked tuning up the transmitter on the trailing wire antenna. Off of that 300 foot long trailing wire, you had a strong signal that you knew would get through without fail. Getting your message received was imperative.

One day we were on a training flight in the eastern part of England. I was practicing sending messages with the trailing wire antenna let out.

All at once I got a red light showing the landing gear down while the trailing wire was still rolled out. We were landing early. We were due to fly two more hours.

I started rolling in that wire on the windup reel but the runway was coming up fast. Would I get my antenna rolled in before we landed? There were trees and houses below. Would that cast iron egg on the end of the antenna hit a tree or would it cave in the side of a house?

I thought I would get it rolled back in on time, but then twang, the windup reel began spinning real fast and about half of my antenna wire and the cast iron egg were gone. I didn't get it rolled in soon enough. The runway beat me to the draw and held the trump card that time.

I sweated it out for three or four days. I was afraid that it might have damaged a house and killed somebody, but I never heard any complaints so I assumed it hit a tree.

Photo courtesy of Dr. J. Howard Cobble

Battle Control Site At 100 BG Airfield

Chapter 43

Brought Bombs Back

Flying back to Thorpe Abbotts on three engines, I got my flimsy sheet out and looked up the secret frequency of a British coastal radio station. I tuned up my radio receiver and transmitter and made my call using Morse International Code. I thought to myself, I sure hope those guys are listening.

I pounded on my key with their call letters and gave them a call. I sure was anxious, but immediately they answered me back. I knew they would, but nevertheless I was relieved when they did.

I gave them the information they needed and they gave me a clearance message in return.

The "Spirit Of Pittwood" took us back to Thorpe Abbotts safely on three engines and we landed with our bombs still hanging there in the racks of the bomb bay.

Before we left the airplane the bomb crew was opening the bomb bay doors and was moving a bomb trailer into position to unload those one thousand pounders.

The next mission for the "Spirit Of Pittwood" would need smaller bombs or incendiaries more than likely.

No credit was given for the 13th mission flown that day. I figured our real 13th mission was still out there waiting for us with red eyes and a big grin.

When we got back to the barracks, "Congratulations you guys, you made it through your 13th mission."

"Hold it, hold all that talk, we didn't make it. We had to turn back. We had to return with two engines out. We got one engine started on the way back and brought our bombs back, so we didn't get credit for the mission."

Nissan Hut

Chapter 44

Gunner Poet

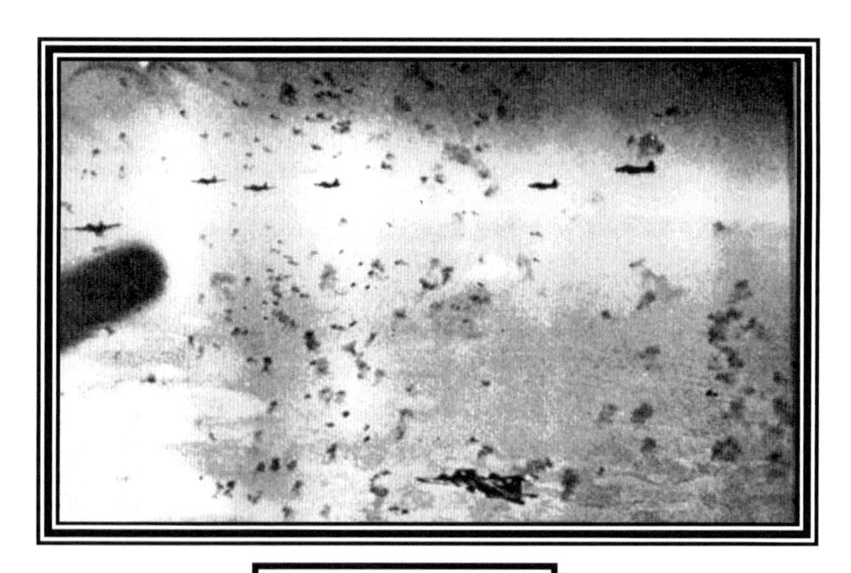

Walking On Flak

Someone from another crew came up to us. "Here I am writing poetry to keep my mind off that piece of flak billowing upwards into our plane with my name on it. But I cannot for the life of me get anyone to listen to one of my poems. How about you guys?"

"No I don't believe so, poems don't appeal to us."

"You guys are going to die tomorrow anyway on your 13th mission, so you might as well listen to one of my poems?"

"Okay, we're not much into poetry, but go ahead and read it to us."

"Thanks a lot, here it goes."

THE COWPOKE GAMBLER

Cowpoke, you quietly left the fray,
You won the prize,
With sparkle in your eyes,
And you happily walked away.

Yes Mister, I'm now on my way,
And you can tell your son,
Cowpoke didn't draw his gun,
He wanted to live another day.

And Mister I know, you are Billie the Kid,
You are tough and smart,
With kindness in your heart,
And of me you are forever rid.

I told my son, he rode over the hill,
Carrying money in his sack,
Luckily for him he never looked back.
Return? No he never will.

I heard someone from the other end of the barracks say, "Curley, don't give up your day job."

That thought also entered my mind, but I didn't want to say anything. He was just writing and using poetry to keep his mind off of his impending death.

Chapter 45

Mission 13 Again

Dangerous Skies

That night I lay on my bunk thinking it all through. We had been awarded an Oak Leaf Cluster to attach to our Air Medal. I also got the fifth stripe for my sleeve.

We had been fortunate. I believed our luck was going to hold. If we could get through this 13th, I believed we would be okay and would complete our 25 missions.

We lost one B-17 on our first 13th mission. When we pulled out of our slot with engine trouble and left the 350th squadron to return to base, another B-17 moved up and took our place.

ROG Farrell J. Davis

I have wondered to this day if that was the B-17 that was lost on the mission. But I never found out about that and it probably was best that I never knew.

The next morning, we got up at 4 o'clock to fly our 13th mission all over again. Working against the clock early in morning there was no time for the number 13 to appear in any of the crewmembers minds.

We went about our work and our preparation for going on a mission in the usual way. We went into briefing and when the Officer pulled the curtain back uncovering the target map, my eyes followed the ribbon from Thorpe Abbotts over to our second 13th mission target and what I saw on that map really surprised me.

Working On Engines

On the day before on our first 13th mission, the bombing results at the canal were poor, so today the 100th was going back to the same target again to finish the job.

They took us out to a different B-17 this time. I don't know what its name was. I don't think it had a name.

This plane today was loaded with six 1000-pound bombs, that being the same bomb load as we had the day before. I figured they would be changing an engine on our "Spirit Of Pittwood" today.

We flew on to the canal target that day and we had very dangerous flak over the target. We dropped our bombs without receiving any damage to the B-17 and returned to Thorpe Abbotts safely. No aircraft were lost in the 100th Bomb Group that day.

The 100th Over An Unknown Target In 1944

Chapter 46

Stand Up Comic

Our crew with a bit less worry was living now with the stress and strain of the 13th mission behind us.

Back in the barracks that night we were talking, laughing and quite happy. Best of all, we were still alive.

We had a break for a day or two so the next day I went over to another barracks to borrow a book to read. Everybody over there was laughing and practically rolling on the floor. What was going on?

I asked my friend, “What’s so funny with those guys?” But then I saw what it was. An awkward skinny guy was standing there with a blank deadpan expression on his face. He was an airman pretend stand-up comic.

No matter what he said, no matter how simple it was, they thought it was hilarious. In their minds he could have gotten a top Vaudeville Stage job in Cleveland.

“What did he say?” I asked.

“His stomach is a hollow log and he’s going to take it to the mess hall and get it slopped.”

That was all right I suppose, but it wasn’t quite funny enough to make me laugh.

While selecting my book the screaming and laughing started up again. “What did he say this time?”

“He dreamed he was awake and when he woke up he was asleep.”

That was kinda funny but not enough to bust a gut over. I picked up my book and started toward the door. As I left I stopped to listen to the guy once more.

“There was smoke in the steamship. The steamship Captain said, “Radioman, send a wire.”

“I couldn’t send a war cuz the wars wuz on far.”

I started walking, time for me to get out of there.

As I walked away the barracks got real quiet. I paused by the window listening and sure enough he came out with another way out joke. It was this.

“I know only two tunes. One of them is Yankee Doodle. The other one isn’t.” I listened no more.

Chapter 47

Death Defined

I believe that facing instant death in combat brings out unknown and hidden qualities lying dormant within a person. I believe I know why a person who knows that he is going to die tomorrow tells jokes and writes poems.

Photo courtesy of Larry Simeone

Wheels Of Rescue

Here is an example. Over in another barracks the ambulance came for a crewmember suffering with a nervous breakdown. He knew he was going to die before the week was out. When they led him out, the young man was covered with sweat from head to foot.

Later, someone came and picked up his clothes. He never returned. I could see by the looks of him and the cold way he stared with unblinking eyes off into nothing that his mind was focused far out on bad.

My thoughts about passing over into another world are probably wrong but here they are. Don't let your mind dwell on death too long. Write pages of poetry, tell jokes, draw pictures, or do anything else you can do. A mind cloaked within itself and left free to run out of control can put you on that slippery slope to ruin.

Drawing Pictures Erases Worry

Chapter 48

The War Goes On

Soon we were back flying missions again and flying in our favorite plane, the B-17 "Spirit Of Pittwood". We flew some rough missions on April 8, 9, 10, and 11.

Two B-17s in our 100th Bomb Group went down on April 10th.

The Spirit Of Pittwood On A Bomb Run

On our Apr. 11th mission, after the bomb drop, we had one bomb left in the bomb bay. It was dangling down on just one hanger. I called the crew on interphone override, "One bomb still in bomb bay hanging on one hanger."

The armorer called on override, "I'll take care of it." The armorer went into the bomb bay and the –40 degree temperature and freezing wind was trying to blow him out of the airplane.

The pilot pulled our B-17 out of the formation and then the armorer started prying on the frozen bomb bracket to make it release.

Usually when a plane pulls out of formation, about four or five FW190s, ME109s and an occasional ME262 jet fighter will attack that B-17 liken unto a swarm of bees and shoot it full of holes. It's not a safe place to be to live a long life and become a grandpa.

Precious Babies

Grandkids: Jonathan, Jennifer, and James

Great Grandkids: Ryan and Rebecca

In about one minute the armorer pried the frozen bomb bracket open and the bomb fell away.

The armorer waved to me and I went on override, “The bomb has dropped, bomb bay clear.”

The pilot closed the bomb bay doors and in one minute he had the “Spirit Of Pittwood” back into the safety of the 350th squadron.

Aircraft Landing March/April 1945

We flew on back to Thorpe Abbotts without any more trouble and landed safely.

Thorpe Abbotts Airfield

Chapter 49

A Few Close Calls

We were flying over villages and farms when that hung up bomb fell. I have often wondered where that single bomb fell and what it hit. Back in the barracks the crew talked about it, but of course we never found out.

Targeting On The Bomb Run

We kept on flying missions until the war ended. Flying missions is hard work and there were a few close calls for our plane but we came through okay.

On one of those last missions, on the bomb run flying in and out of the clouds, we were coming up on the target.

I had the radio room door opened and was standing in the door watching the bombs that were ready to start falling out at any second.

Heading For Home

All at once our B-17 commenced bouncing and rocking in extreme turbulence. It would throw me up and then fall out from under me. I was hanging on for dear life, as I didn't want to fall out with the bombs. I suppose it could be characterized as tumultuous.

I looked up and saw a squadron of about a dozen planes, flying on their own bomb run heading. They were flying about 200 feet above us. They were flying across our squadron at an angle toward a different section of the target. I saw bombs hanging in their open bomb bays above us about ready to be dropped.

They flew on past us and in about two seconds their bombs began falling. At the same time our bombs began falling away also. Needless to say, I was scared and at a cold –40 degrees below zero, I was sweating icicles. Back on the ground at Thorpe Abbotts, no one said anything about the incident. It was just something normally encountered in a day's work I suppose.

Trailer At The End Of Runway
Housing Radio Equipment

Chapter 50

V E Day

When the hostilities ended we had completed 20 missions. You needed 25 completed missions to return to the U.S. (ZOI) and home. With only 20 missions we had more aircrew time ahead and more flying to do.

The war in Europe was over but we were still soldiers in the US Army Air Corps. To keep us busy they found all kind of work and tasks for everyone to do.

Solid Silver World War II Souvenir

Since I had five stripes on my sleeve, they put me in charge of the barracks. It was my job to see that everyone kept their living area clean and orderly.

Every two or three days our crew was called upon to fly out of England to someplace over on the continent. Here are some of the flights we made.

Loading Up POWs

We flew to pick up POWs and laborers in Austria, and took them to Chartres, France, close to Paris, where they got on trucks and went home. It was hard for them to realize their good fortune. In one's life, the greatness for a prisoner to be reprieved, especially from that of eminent death is a grand feeling.

Every one was given a parachute to wear. As I helped a man adjust his parachute harness, he took out of his pocket a handful of silver coins. Smiling at me with happiness and joy, he picked out two beautiful silver coins and gave them to me. I still have those coins.

Potsdam Church Coin

Paul Von Hindenburg Coin

Later when we were getting on the plane to fly back to Thorpe Abbotts, England, the pilot and co-pilot said, “We are going to fly low and take a look at Paris.” They did! We flew so low over Paris that I looked up and saw people in the top of the Eiffel Tower watching us fly by below.

Some other flights: We were called upon to fly a General and his staff to various cities on inspection trips.

We flew on the first food drop mission to Holland as the camera ship. These flights were called chowhound missions.

We made one or more flights down to the south German area.

Chowhound Missions To Holland

Chapter 51

A Load Of Money

We flew to North Africa hauling footlockers packed full of Army records.

"What's in those footlockers?" Someone asked us.

"We were told they're full of Army records." I replied.

"You don't think the big Army Headquarters in London is going to send their valuable records off to North Africa, where there is nothing, do you?"

"I don't know."

"I'll tell you what's in those footlockers."

"What is it?" Now, he had me curious.

"It's money. The soldiers need money to get paid every month. You have a plane load of money."

It didn't matter to me one way or the other, but down through the years I've often thought about those foot-lockers. It might have been money, I never knew.

Chapter 52

The Scrap Pile

In December 1945 our “Spirit Of Pittwood” returned to the U.S.

Our Spirit Of Pittwood was not famous as the likes of The Memphis Belle, Hard Luck, Squawking Hawk, Laden Maden, Fletchers Castoria and others. However, our pilot, Lt. Milton Alvo and co-pilot, Lt. David Tallichet were famous in our eyes. We had many close calls and they always knew what action to take and exactly what to do. Their expertise and skill pulled us through many tight spots.

The “Spirit” as we called our favorite airplane, finally ended up in the aircraft boneyard in Kingman, Arizona to be parked for a long time and then sold for scrap.

“Skipper II” was sent to the Kingman boneyard also with the same fate ahead of it. “Baby Bunty” didn’t make it back to the U.S. It was scrapped overseas someplace.

I always hoped the “Spirit Of Pittwood” would be bought by a museum where I could go and see it again, but I don’t think it ever was.

I think there were more B-17’s parked out west in Kingman and other Air Bases than Carter had pills.

Chapter 53

A Change Of Venue

One day a Sergeant came into the barracks and called out. "T/Sgt. Davis, aircrew radioman, T/Sgt. Bitel, aircrew engineer."

"Here we are."

"Both of you men are leaving the Eighth Air Force and you have been assigned to HQ & HQ Squadron, USAFE." (United States Air Forces in Europe). "Here are your orders."

"Pack your bags at once. In an hour a vehicle will be by to take you to the train station in Diss. You have ticket vouchers to London. When you get to London, check in with the ATC, the Air Transport Command, for a plane to Frankfurt, Germany. Someone will meet you in Frankfurt with further instructions."

"Sergeant, what's this all about?" Bitel asked.

"There's a B-17 on an airport down below Frankfurt close to Munich and they are making up a crew to fly a valuable cargo to the United States. They called for the most experienced and qualified men available and you two were chosen."

Bitel and I said goodbye to our pilot Lt. Milton Alvo and to our co-pilot Lt. David Tallichet and also to the rest of the aircrew, leaving the crew and going on our way, never to see any of them again in our lifetimes.

Lt. David Tallichet died October 2007 at 84 years of age.

Soon we were riding on the train, going to London, Frankfurt and beyond. We had a new life with new duties and adventures on ahead in the USAFE.

A Village In England

Chapter 54

Going Home

Outside our barracks, Bitel and Davis (front row) saying good-bye with a picture to remember.

It was hard for my mind, modified to war, to accept the fact that the war was over and we were going home.

In London we spent the night at a Red Cross club. They charged us 75 cents for the room.

The next morning at the airport we went to the ATC (Air Transport Command) counter to get on a flight. "I'm sorry, there's nothing available to Frankfurt. It will be several days before any space becomes available."

That afternoon I ran across a friend of mine who was in a class with me back at the Univ. of Missouri CTD. He was now the radioman on an aircrew flying the huge B-29 super bomber from the U.S. to London to Frankfurt. In the morning they were flying on to Frankfurt. We asked for a ride. Begged might be a better word!

He checked with his pilot and got clearance for us. Early the next morning we were flying in that B-29 and on our way to Frankfurt.

In Frankfurt some facts were revealed to us. Down at an airfield in Germany, Oberphafenhofen, close to Munich, they were waiting for an aircrew to arrive that had been ordered. Farrell Davis was flying as radioman on that aircrew. Boleslaw Bitel was to fly as engineer.

We hoped the rest of the crew; a pilot, co- pilot and navigator were experienced and knew how to fly the Atlantic. No need for worry, they were young, but highly accomplished and experienced, we found out later.

Chapter 55

Flying The Atlantic

When we flew the north Atlantic delivering a new B-17 from the U.S over to the U.K., our aircrew had no trouble.

However, a B-17 ahead of us missed Iceland and flew on out into the Atlantic. No radio message was ever received and they were never found.

The BC-375 transmitter and the BC-348 receiver were standard in every B-17 radio room. On the BC-375 transmitter, voice was only good for about 200 or 300 miles. CW was good for about 700 or 800 miles.

Flying the Atlantic, if you got lost, sending a Morse code SOS on CW might cover the distance to a rescue ship. A Mayday sent out on voice might not be heard through the static.

USA Bound

Chapter 56

Travel In Germany

It took about a week of stop and go surface travel for us to get from Frankfurt down to our destination, Oberphafenhofen Air Base, the German airfield where our plane was waiting. I acquired some interesting souvenirs along the way.

Eagle Clutching Swastika

There was valuable cargo en route from an unknown place, unknown to me that is, to be loaded on the plane. I never knew what that valuable cargo was.

In a few days the rest of the crew arrived at Ober, but it was several more days before the cargo arrived to be loaded in the B-17's bomb bay.

The following morning with the valuable cargo on board and secure, with several military passengers on board, we left out early on our flight from Oberphafenhofen Air Base in Germany to the United States.

Souvenirs

German And English Souvenirs

Chapter 57

Europe To America

The pilot received his list of airports, tower radio frequencies, etc. I received my list of call letters and frequencies of radio stations along our flight path. I was required to call in position reports on Morse Code (CW) along the way, especially when flying across the Atlantic.

On the way home our route of travel was as follows: (I should have written this down many years ago). Rome, Italy – Algiers, Algeria – Casablanca, Morocco - Dakar, Senegal French West Africa – Natal or Recife, Brazil – Georgetown, British Guiana – Ramey AFB, Puerto Rico – Morrison Field, West Palm Beach, Florida.

Everyone shopped for souvenirs at each stop along the way. I had a goodly amount of money when we left London but I spent most of it on my way down from Frankfurt to Ober.

I scraped up enough money to buy a wooden sculpture, a handmade souvenir from Casablanca, called Little Woman.

At Morrison Field, the crew shook hands all around and then everyone went on their own separate ways. They shipped me out to Maxwell AFB, Alabama.

You may wonder how my young friends back at the Martha Berry School fared? All of them didn't survive the war. I feel bad about losing some of my good friends.

I'm happy to say though that one of those friends did get the gold bars to wear on his shoulders.

And as for me, well, I was commissioned a 2nd Lt. and finally received those gold bars to wear on my own shoulders . . . But that is another story.

The End

I hope you enjoyed this account of my life during the Great Depression and World War II. I have relished the journey through my past experiences both good and bad. I hope I have brought you good memories and enlightenment as well as encouraging tales.

Sincerely,

Timberline Davis

An author feels gloriously peaceful and wonderfully released when the book he is writing is finally finished and put to bed.

You have finished reading this account. I know there are those of you who are special people, having inquisitive minds and a daring spirit. If you seek new adventures, I invite you to travel with me through time and space and enter the Portal to a strange and neglected land.

Come journey with me on alien roads along with handsome Gary Hathaway and beautiful Katherine Lane as they live for 300 years in a mystic land filled with snarling, treacherous, snake-eye people.

Find true adventure in a pink land located way beyond the sunset. It's all to be found in my exciting fantasy novel, ***THE LAND OF NEGLECT.*** Available at amazon.com

Dedication

To my wife, Juanita Pearl Elliott Davis, who has been suffering through an illness. She has sat silently and smiled at me as I worked. Juanita Pearl has been at my side through thick and thin for 68 years.

Acknowledgments

No author writes a book in reclusive isolation. All writers have many people to thank and I am no different.

Thanks to the following who have given their valuable time and have helped me with the work.

My sincere gratitude to Barry Davis, Gregory Davis, Amber Pickle, Beverly Bruemmer, Stan Paschal, Hamp Dobbs, Sandra Mayfield, and Jaime Sasser.

World War II Pictures

Courtesy of: 100th BOMB GROUP FOUNDATION

With special thanks to: Carol Tallichet, M.P. Faley, Jan Riddling and Cindy Goodman.

Also special thanks to: Dr. J. Howard Cobble.

A TRULY INSPIRING

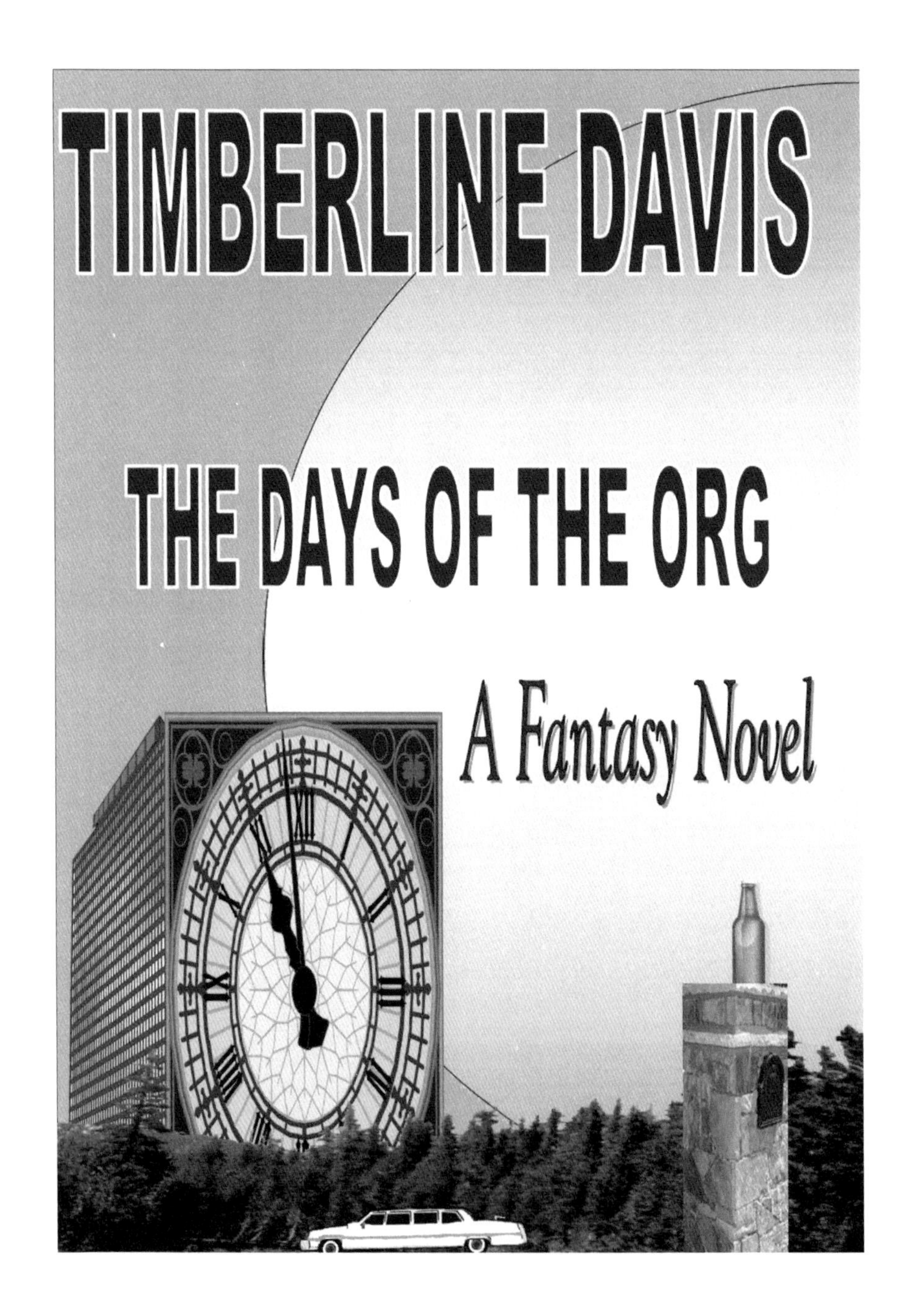

FANTASY NOVEL

CONTINUE THE FANTASY

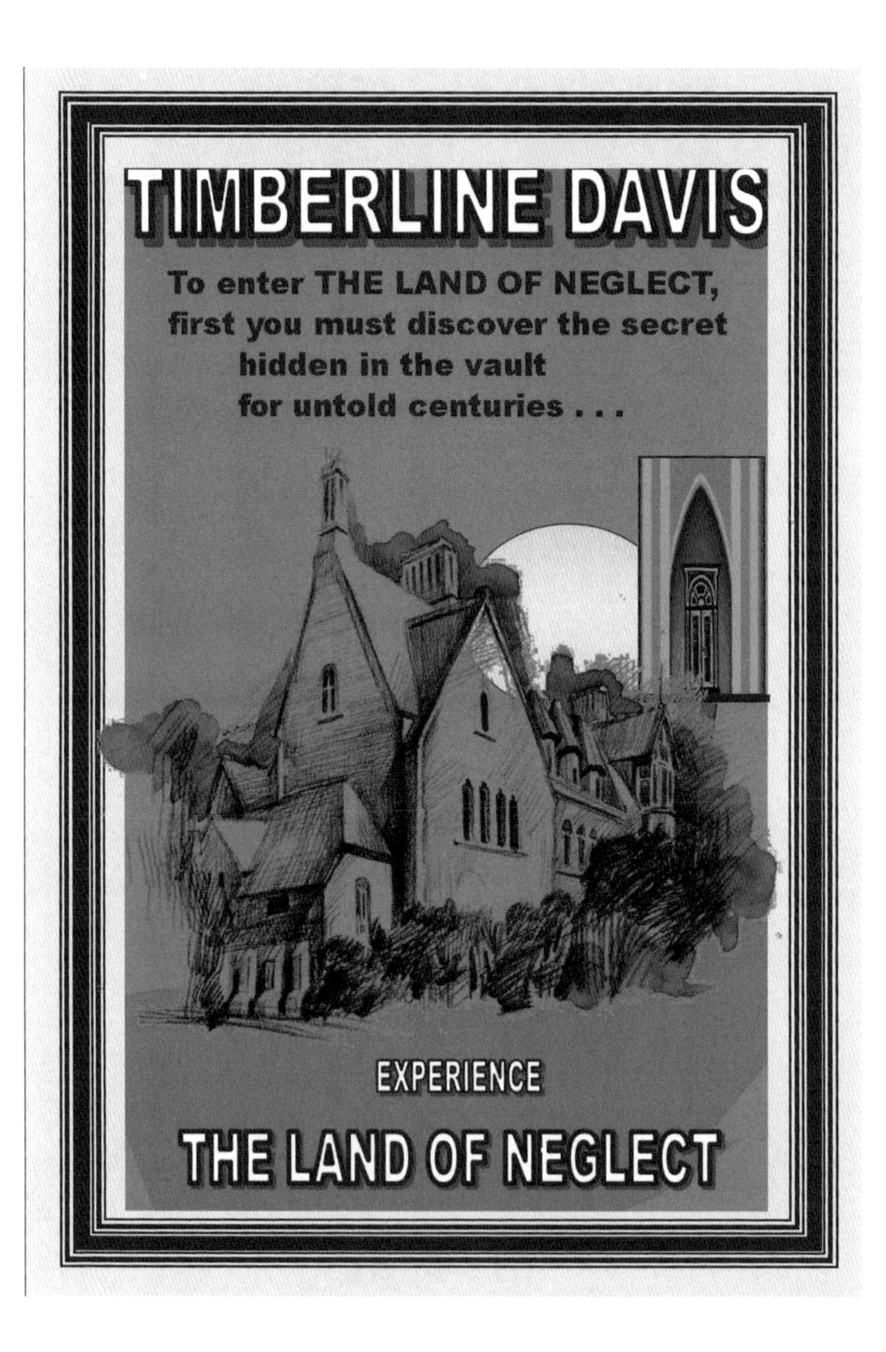

IN THIS SEQUEL

COMING SOON

TIMBERLINE DAVIS
UNDER THE MAGIC
CHESTNUT TREES
THE PATH SEEKERS
BEVERLY BRUEMMER

About The Author

After serving in the war, Farrell J. Davis took his skills and love of aircraft to commercial airlines for over thirty years. He utilized his FCC General Radio license for weather radar and radio communications coast to coast.

Ever resourceful and energetic, Mr. Davis acquired a 150 acre farm. He raised cattle and bees, built houses performing the necessary trades himself, and sold the many antiques he had collected over the years while trading in stocks, options, and commodity futures.

His incredible imagination coupled with life experiences compelled him to create characters and worlds that took on a life of their own. Author of two fantasy novels, *The Days Of The Org*, and *The Land Of Neglect,* Timberline Davis shares his past with us in, ***13***, an autobiography dedicated to his loving wife and family.

WGRL-HQ BIOGRAPHY
31057102176024
BIO DAVIS ADV
Davis, Earnest
Timberline Davis : the life
and times of Farrell J. Davi

2/18